SOARING ABOVE THE CIRCUMSTANCES

Dean Kilmer

SOARING
ABOVE THE
CIRCUMSTANCES

VICTORIOUS LIVING
IN SPITE OF ILLNESS OR STRESS

© 2015 by Dean Kilmer

All rights reserved. No part of this publication may be reproduced, stored in a retrieval system, or transmitted in any form or by any means without the prior written permission of the author. The only exception is brief quotations in printed reviews.

ISBN-10: 1941972748
ISBN-13: 978-1941972748

Library of Congress Control Number: 2015954808

Published by Start2Finish Books
PO Box 660675 #54705
Dallas, TX 75266-0675
www.start2finish.org

Printed in the United States of America

Unless otherwise noted, all Scripture quotations are from The Holy Bible, English Standard Version®, copyright © 2001 by Crossway Bibles, a publishing ministry of Good News Publishers. Used by permission. All rights reserved.

Scripture quotations marked NIV are from HOLY BIBLE, NEW INTERNATIONAL VERSION®. Copyright © 1973, 1978, 1984 by International Bible Society. Used by permission of Zondervan Publishing House.

Cover Design: Josh Feit, Evangela.com

DEDICATION

To my many heroes of faith in the Brown Street church who have soared above their circumstances and inspired others to grow in faith.

TABLE OF CONTENTS

Learning to Soar Above Your Circumstances	**9**
My Heroes of Faith	11
Soaring Above Your Circumstances	21
The Moment You Can Never Forget	32
Not Me!	44
Do I Really Know What I'm Doing?	51

True Stories of Soaring Above Suffering	**60**
Ninety-Three Years Old, Smiling and Happy	62
A Soul Thirsty for God	69
What Do You Do When Your World is Turned Upside-Down?	74
The Serendipity of Suffering	82
The Doctor Refused to Look Her in the Eye	92
A Good Heart and an Unexpected Blessing	101

Biblical Power to Soar Above Your Struggles	**105**
Strength When Your Prayers Are Not Answered	107
When You're Completely Helpless, Look Toward God	112
Christ In You, the Hope of Glory	121
A Beautiful, Beautiful Pain-Free Day	129

PART 1:

LEARNING TO SOAR ABOVE YOUR CIRCUMSTANCES

1

MY HEROES OF FAITH

Not only that, but we rejoice in our sufferings, knowing that suffering produces endurance, and endurance produces character, and character produces hope, and hope does not put us to shame, because God's love has been poured into our hearts through the Holy Spirit who has been given to us.

Romans 5:3-5

On Sundays, I have the privilege of preaching for the Brown Street Church of Christ in Waxahachie, Texas. Everywhere I look, I see the evidence of faith's life-changing power. Throughout the sanctuary, there are people who are weary from years of fighting serious illnesses and yet are living victoriously. As I sit on the small pew located on the left-hand side of the podium, I look out over the congregation...

When I look into the first section on my left, my eyes fall on Jan Jackson and her husband, Tommy. Although she has had a series of back surgeries and is in constant pain, Jan has a pleasant expression on her face as she worships God. Because of the relentless pain, there are times when she is forced to stand up at the back of the auditorium; the pain simply won't allow her to sit comfortably. In spite of her pain, Jan and Tommy often entertain members of our church family in their home. She is a gracious hostess who never complains about her pain. As I look at her, I am reminded of the power of great faith.

As my eyes swing to the right, in the next section, Loyce Campbell is seated about halfway back with a warm, friendly smile on her face. Looking at that smile, you would never guess that her husband, Gene, battled cancer for almost ten years. During those ten years, Gene served as a shepherd for our church family. Gene's story is in chapter 7.

In the back of that same section, Tom Ford, a tall, strong man, sits by himself and worships God. His wife, Anne, is in the hospital recovering from a stem cell transplant. Her battle with cancer over the past several years has made her unable to eat solid food. Even so, she often prepares meals for those who have lost loved ones and for the shut-ins of the church. She's a marvelous cook who enjoys serving others while she remains on a liquid diet. When she is able to attend worship service, her smile carries a radiant glow. Read more about Anne in chapter 10.

A few rows in front of the Fords, Paul and Susan O'Rear are entering into the worship service. I have often referred to Paul as the "heart and soul" of our congregation. He is a big man with a booming voice and a laugh that echoes throughout our building. Paul is not seated in one of the pews; he is in his motorized chair. For over ten years, Paul has battled a vitamin B-12 deficiency, which sometimes makes it impossible for him to walk. Laughing, encouraging, building others' faith, and almost never complaining, Paul represents the best of Christian faith. Everyone is inspired by his presence! One Sunday, we had a great time in the foyer of the church when Paul and Annita Patterson had a race in their motorized chairs. What great fun! They were uplifting others and rejoicing in their weakness. I know you will enjoy chapter 9, which was written by Paul himself.

For when I am weak, then I am strong.

2 Corinthians 12:10

As my eyes move one more section to the right, at the very back I focus in on Kenneth Kirk, a big, strong man who sits with his arm around his wife and a big smile on his face. He seems to always smile and is positive and encouraging when he speaks. He often talks about his blessings. On occasions, I notice that his coloring is paler than usual, and I realize that his radiation treatments have affected his strength. However, I have never once heard him complain or act as if he were struggling. Kenneth understands and rejoices in the fact that God has an eternal plan.

> So we do not lose heart. Though our outer self is wasting away, our inner self is being renewed day by day. For this light momentary affliction is preparing for us an eternal weight of glory beyond all comparison.
>
> 2 Corinthians 4:16-17

A few rows in front of Kenneth sits Anne Schroeder, a thin, smiling lady who brings joy to everyone around her. With a big smile, she reminds people to "beware of the skinny cook," referring to herself. Anne is always preparing meals for those in need despite her own long struggle with cancer. She lost her daughter to cancer a few years back and her husband to heart disease not long afterward. Does she spend time complaining or blaming God? Not a chance! Her faith is solid as a rock! If you ever need help with anything, Anne is ready to volunteer.

> Then the King will say to those on his right, "Come, you who are blessed by my Father, inherit the kingdom prepared for you from the foundation of the world. For I was hungry and you gave me food, I was thirsty and you gave me drink, I was a stranger and you welcomed me."
>
> Matthew 25:34-35

As my eyes move one more section to the right, I see Donna Conn smiling and wearing a stylish hat to cover up the fact that chemotherapy has taken her red hair. Her seven-year-old grandson, Ethan, sits smiling beside her. Donna is the major influence in his young life. He's one of my favorite kids because he loves to pick up attendance cards and always wants to shake my hand after services. At times Donna looks very pale during worship service, but she is diligently fulfilling her mission to help Ethan grow up to love God.

But Jesus said, "Let the little children come to me and do not hinder them, for to such belongs the kingdom of heaven."

Matthew 19:14

A few rows back, Susan Walden and Sarah Fletcher are with their families; both are cancer survivors. I rarely see either one of them without a smile and some exciting story to tell about their children. Godly children are the result of courageous, faithful parents. Susan's oldest son is now in medical school, planning to spend his career working on a cure for cancer.

Not only that, but we rejoice in our sufferings, knowing that suffering produces endurance, and endurance produces character, and character produces hope, and hope does not put us to shame, because God's love has been poured into our hearts through the Holy Spirit who has been given to us.

Romans 5:3-5

When my eyes travel to the last section of the auditorium, I see another friendly face: that of Robin Phillips, who recently lost her husband and has struggled with financial issues since his death. As if that weren't enough, she fractured her leg and has been unable to put any weight on it for the last three months, and yet she smiles and is a blessing to others. Robin shares her experiences in chapter 8.

These people have some important characteristics in common:

1. They all inspire others with their faith and actions.
2. They all have great faith in God.
3. They all are involved in serving other people in spite of their problems.
4. They all know that God has a purpose for their lives.

As you prepare for great service to God during the rest of your life, please consider the following passages of Scripture and keep in mind who wrote them. Mark your favorite thoughts from each passage below. Then take a moment to quietly be thankful.

From the apostle Paul:

I can do all things through him who strengthens me.

Philippians 4:13

Brothers, I do not consider that I have made it my own. But one thing I do: forgetting what lies behind and straining forward to what lies ahead, I press on toward the goal for the prize of the upward call of God in Christ Jesus.

Philippians 3:13-14

No, in all these things we are more than conquerors through him who loved us. For I am sure that neither death nor life, nor angels nor rulers, nor things present nor things to come, nor powers, nor height nor depth, nor anything else in all creation, will be able to separate us from the love of God in Christ Jesus our Lord.

Romans 8:37-39

Now, take a moment to be thankful that you never suffered the way Paul suffered. I'm thankful that I've never been stoned and left for dead. I'm thankful that I've never been put in prison for years. I'm thankful that I've never suffered a Roman beating.

From Jonah:

I called out to the Lord, out of my distress, and he answered me; out of the belly of Sheol I cried, and you heard my voice.

Jonah 2:2

When my life was fainting away, I remembered the Lord, and my prayer came to you, into your holy temple (Jonah 2:7).

And the Lord spoke to the fish, and it vomited Jonah out upon the dry land.

Jonah 2:10

Take a moment to be thankful; you have never been in the belly of a whale! You have never been as far away from God as Jonah was during this prayer.

From David:

The Lord is my shepherd; I shall not want. He makes me lie down in green pastures. He leads me beside still waters. He restores my soul. He leads me in paths of righteousness for his name's sake. Even though I walk through the valley of the shadow of death, I will fear no evil, for you are with me; your rod and your staff, they comfort me.

Psalm 23:1-4

Blessed is the man who walks not in the counsel of the wicked, nor stands in the way of sinners, nor sits in the seat of scoffers; but his delight is in the law of the Lord, and on his law he meditates day and night.

Psalm 1:1-2

Your word is a lamp to my feet and a light to my path.

> Psalm 119:105

Give thanks to the Lord, for he is good, for his steadfast love endures forever.

> Psalm 136:1

Take a moment to be thankful for the fact that you've never had a son who would lead an army in rebellion against you, as David had to endure (2 Samuel 18).

2

SOARING ABOVE YOUR CIRCUMSTANCES

> Do not be anxious about anything, but in everything by prayer and supplication with thanksgiving let your requests be made known to God. And the peace of God, which surpasses all understanding, will guard your hearts and your minds in Christ Jesus.
>
> Philippians 4:6-7

More than 117 million people in our country are living with chronic illnesses. Taking into account their family members who provide them with care, almost everyone in our country is dealing with some form of serious illness. How can we find joy under these circumstances? The answer comes from our Savior, Jesus Christ, and our ability to understand His marvelous grace and His awesome power. As Christians who are living for Christ, we do not live under our circumstances; rather, like eagles, we are able to soar above our circumstances. His power and love gently lift us above the storms of our suffering. When a storm is approaching, an eagle immediately finds a high perch and waits for the winds to arrive. As soon as they do, the eagle spreads its wings and glides gracefully higher until it is above the storm. The eagle does not fight the storm; it uses the wind to climb to safety. We need to learn not to be distressed by our illnesses; instead, we can use our struggles to fly closer to our God.

DON'T LOOK DOWN AT YOUR PROBLEMS; LOOK UP AT THE GOD WHO LOVES YOU!

Blessed be the God and Father of our Lord Jesus Christ, the Father of mercies and God of all comfort, who comforts us in all our affliction, so that we may be able to comfort those who are in any affliction, with the comfort with which we ourselves are comforted by God.

2 Corinthians 1:3-4

Just as the eagle uses the storm's power to draw higher, we can use the destructive power of illness to lift our faith higher until the grace of God takes control of our hearts. At that moment, we begin to see His power working in our lives.

> But they who wait for the Lord shall renew their strength; they shall mount up with wings like eagles; they shall run and not be weary; they shall walk and not faint.
>
> Isaiah 40:31

God's mighty power renews our spiritual strength and ignites the eternal purpose in our inner being.

> For this light momentary affliction is preparing for us an eternal weight of glory beyond all comparison.
>
> 2 Corinthians 4:17

"Beyond all comparison"—I love that thought! I cannot see the glory of God working in my pain, but I can be sure that nothing I experience now even compares with the beauty of my heavenly home. God is and has always been above the circumstances of our lives. If we live for Him, He has an eternal plan that includes a reward in heaven. His home provides an eternity without pain or suffering. He gives us a home which is imperishable, undefiled, and unfading. Read with joy and anticipation Peter's comments about our future glorious home with God:

> Blessed be the God and Father of our Lord Jesus Christ! According to his great mercy, he has caused us to be born again to a living hope through the resurrection of Jesus Christ from the dead, to an inheritance that is imperishable, undefiled, and unfading, kept in heaven for you, who by God's power are being guarded through faith for a salvation ready to be revealed in the last time. In this you rejoice, though now for a little while, if necessary, you have been grieved by various trials, so that the tested genuineness of your faith—more precious than gold that perishes though it is tested by fire—may be found to result in praise and glory and honor at the revelation of Jesus Christ.
>
> 1 Peter 1:3-7

DON'T LOOK AT WHAT YOU CANNOT DO; LOOK AT WHAT YOU CAN ACCOMPLISH IN CHRIST!

I can do all things through him who strengthens me.

Philippians 4:13

The apostle Paul was imprisoned when he wrote those words. He was growing old; he had a thorn in the flesh, which was probably blindness, and his body had been torn by beatings. He had even been stoned and left for dead. He could not leave his prison cell, and his body was completely worn out. Yet from that dreadful prison cell, he wrote some of the most powerful books in the New Testament. He wasn't looking at what he could not do; he was allowing God to work in him! What can God do with you? Are you a light to all those around you? Are they amazed by your great faith? Are they uplifted by your courage? You can be a life-changing light for others regardless of your circumstances!

This book is full of stories of real people who, like Paul, have discovered the secret of how to rise above the difficult circumstances of their lives. That secret lies in shifting the focus away from our suffering as we look for ways to bless other people. Investing our lives in other people allows God to radiate His glory through us!

What are the possibilities in your life if you allow Christ to control your heart and your future? How high can you soar with Jesus lifting you heavenward?

PAUL DIDN'T LOOK AT THE ABUNDANCE OF SUFFERING; HE LOOKED AT THE ABUNDANCE OF COMFORT!

> For as we share abundantly in Christ's sufferings, so through Christ we share abundantly in comfort too. If we are afflicted, it is for your comfort and salvation; and if we are comforted, it is for your comfort, which you experience when you patiently endure the same sufferings that we suffer. Our hope for you is unshaken, for we know that as you share in our sufferings, you will also share in our comfort.
>
> 2 Corinthians 1:5-7

There is a help, a peace, an assurance, and a soothing relaxation that come to those who know they belong to God.

> And let the peace of Christ rule in your hearts, to which indeed you were called in one body. And be thankful.
>
> Colossians 3:15

Our attitude about our circumstances is much more important than the circumstances themselves. God provides the exact amount of strength and comfort we need. As I sometimes like to say, attitude is more important than reality! This is especially true when we consider the struggles of our lives. Helen Keller once said, "Character cannot be developed in ease and quiet. Only through experience, trial and suffering can the soul be strengthened, ambition inspired, and success achieved."

You are probably thinking that you would rather not have to suffer in order to accomplish something great. However, because you are suffering, use God's power to accomplish something extraordinary in your life.

Not only can an eagle soar above the storm, but it also has been blessed by God with great eyesight. An eagle has the ability to spot its intended target from high in the sky. Soar like an eagle and use your spiritual vision to see what God has planned. You have been blessed with a unique personality, unique opportunities and unique talents. You have opportunities that no one else in the world can claim. Glorify God as you look with eagles' eyes to see your purpose.

WHEN YOU CAN'T UNDERSTAND WHY, ASK, "WHO IS IN CHARGE?"

Joseph's great dreams of success and power were destroyed in one afternoon when his brothers violently attacked him. At first, they were going to kill him, but they realized they could make some money by selling him into slavery. His own brothers sold him! Can you imagine the pain? Can you comprehend the mental anguish? If you were Joseph, how angry would you be? How hurt would you be? How many ways would your mind invent to get revenge? It wouldn't take long to be completely filled with hate! Did you feel angry and betrayed by God when you first learned of your illness? If so, take a close look at Joseph's response to his circumstances.

It seems only human that Joseph would continue to grow in anger and resentment during the seventeen years he spent as a slave and then in prison, but instead he continued to glorify God through his actions. He did not allow himself to get "under the circumstances." During his time in slavery, he became the best slave in Potiphar's house. Don't you think that being forced into prison without just cause should have been another step into despair? Not for Joseph! He became a trusted servant to the jailer. Joseph was able to endure all his suffering for only one reason: he had confidence that God was in charge of the circumstances! In all those years, he must have wondered what God had in mind for his life. However, his trust in God brought him back to that one powerful thought and allowed him to forgive his brothers and save his family from starvation. Listen carefully to what Joseph says when he reveals himself to his brothers:

> So Joseph said to his brothers, "Come near to me, please." And they came near. And he said, "I am your brother, Joseph, whom you sold into Egypt. And now do not be distressed or angry with yourselves because you sold me here, for God sent me before you to preserve life."
>
> Genesis 45:4-5

We must never doubt the fact that God is in charge! Yes, our pain may be great and our struggles severe, but we must have confidence that God is in control. As long as we are willing to follow His path, victory and rejoicing await every single one of us! His Son has given us eternal life, and we can confidently rejoice even in pain and suffering.

YOU CAN FLY PEACEFULLY ABOVE THE CIRCUMSTANCES OF YOUR LIFE!

The rest of this book shares the secret I have learned that has helped many Christians to soar above the circumstances of our chronic illnesses. Blessing the lives of others in spite of our suffering—in simple terms, that's the secret. As I personally have lived with diabetes for fifty years, I have been inspired by witnessing the faithful lives of many brothers and sisters whose testimonies you will read about in the chapters to come.

Consider the following ways to live above your circumstances. Please mark the things below that you can do. You may be amazed at what God can do through your life.

- I can make telephone calls to encourage others.
- I can speak gently to others when I'm in a doctor's office.
- I can become a teacher for correspondence Bible studies such as World Bible School.
- I can prepare meals for those who have lost loved ones.
- I can attend worship service and be an example to others.

- I can encourage the leaders of the church.
- I can be a strong example for my own family.
- I can write cards to those who are suffering.
- I can spend time in prayer for other people.

3

THE MOMENT YOU CAN NEVER FORGET

And David said, "The Lord who delivered me from the paw of the lion and from the paw of the bear will deliver me from the hand of this Philistine..."

1 Samuel 17:37

I'm confident that David never forgot the day he stepped into the valley to face the nine-foot giant, Goliath. His heart would have been pounding, his breath heavy, his muscles tense, as he looked up into the eyes of a killer. Could he survive this battle? His life would never be the same. He would either die on that battle field, or he would become God's man and a hero to his people.

There is no other moment like it! You come in to see your doctor for a regular checkup, and suddenly you face a giant of huge proportions. The doctor has called you back in for additional tests. At this point, you have questions, but don't really believe anything serious is wrong. It is at this moment that the doctor explains that you have a brain tumor, and that it could be malignant. Your whole body goes numb, and your mind begins to race; your heart is pounding, your muscles tense. There must be something wrong. Surely he's not talking about me. Is it possible I could die? What am I going to tell my family? What about all the things I had planned? I don't understand why this is happening to me. Am I going to survive? Will I have a normal life?

It really makes no difference whether the doctor says the problem is a brain tumor, cancer, heart failure, Lou Gehrig's disease, or any other life-changing disease; reactions are much the same. The feeling in the pit of your stomach is nauseating. You struggle to find words. What questions should I ask? Can I get a second opinion? It's a horrible nightmare, but you're awake. As the doctor continues this talk, you struggle to understand.

When you leave the doctor's office, you have trouble focusing. Now comes the time for a long discussion with your family. What should you tell them? You pick up the phone to call your kids and set it back down, unsure of what to say.

When the shock wears off, the real depth of the diagnosis begins to set in. Now you have some choices to make. Will you give up on life and simply endure the time you have left, feeling sorry for yourself? Will you start planning your own funeral and saying goodbye to all your loved ones? Or will you live out every day of your life with the victory of faith? The reality is that you're not dead yet! Whether your disease is a short-term critical illness or a slow killer such as diabetes, you still have a choice! To all of us who have chronic illnesses, I suggest we stop feeling sorry for ourselves and rejoice in the future God will provide for us.

As we continue through this examination of victory in the midst of a critical illness, we will consider some people who have enjoyed meaningful, victorious lives with both short-term and long-term illnesses. We will also look at the great blessing to be found in the lives of those of us who deal with chronic illness. I'm sorry if it shocked you when I used the term "blessing" in the same sentence with "chronic illness." I can honestly say that I've been blessed with type I diabetes, which at the present time is the number three killer in the United States. In my own life, I have come to realize that God has blessed me in many special ways because of my illness. First, because of my strict requirement to eat at specific times, our family has always enjoyed meals together. As our children were growing up, this became a wonderful time of communication, sharing, and laughter. A second blessing came in the form of the great love demonstrated by my wife and children during the difficult times when I suffered severe complications of diabetes. Love grows stronger during times of struggle! A third great blessing has come in my ministry: Because of my health problems, I have learned to sympathize with others who have health issues. Equally important is the fact that I have learned to rely more on God's strength and love. Throughout the rest of this book, you will be surprised by the lives of many other individuals with short-term critical illnesses and the joy they have discovered during their illnesses.

THE DAY I THOUGHT I WAS GOING TO DIE

As you read the above statement, you probably assumed I was expecting to die as a result of my diabetes. You would be completely wrong. On a March day in 1965, I thought I was going to die as a result of laziness. Yep, I was pronounced a lazy kid. My father was a wonderful man; he loved his family with all his heart. However, as a World War II veteran and a captain in the National Guard, he was also a strict disciplinarian. As far as Bud Kilmer was concerned, one of the worst crimes you could commit was being lazy. The trouble started when I was declared an absolutely lazy kid!

Oh man, was I in trouble! During my sophomore year of high school, I was falling asleep in classes at school. Almost as bad, I was neglecting many of the things I was expected to do at home. I came home tired and crashed early almost every night. I convinced good old Mom that something had to be wrong, so she took me to see Dr. Travis, our long-time family doctor. In the 1960s, country doctors didn't look for diabetes very often, especially among healthy-looking teenagers. Sixteen years earlier Dr. Travis had been there at my birth; he had known me all my life. After a quick check of my heart and blood pressure he simply said, "There's nothing wrong with this boy; he's just lazy." Needless to say, Dad was not happy. I was getting in deeper every day, and it was going to get a lot worse!

For the next six months, I did everything I could to prove I was not a lazy kid. However, it just wasn't working; I felt awful and had no energy at all. When a new doctor moved to town there was an emphatic debate between my mother and father.

Mom, bless her heart, was convinced there was something wrong with me. Money was in short supply, so Dad was not interested in paying another doctor to do a series of expensive tests. As I continued to get worse, my mother finally prevailed, and we went to the new doctor. Believe it or not, I had high hopes that he would find something wrong with me!

Being new in town and wanting to increase his patient load, he was extremely thorough. It seemed that we went through every possible test in the next two days. As he looked directly into my mother's eyes, he gave us the shocking conclusion: "There's nothing wrong with this boy; he's just lazy." At that moment, I knew I was dead! I didn't know what Dad would do when he heard the condemning news, but I was sure that after wasting all that money for an extensive checkup, he would be red-faced, his hands would be sweaty, and his voice would be loud. It sure looked bleak! Honestly, I really, really, really wanted that doctor to find something wrong with me. After all, being sick was my only hope for survival! Any illness would be better than watching my father explode. Something quick and easily solved would be best, but anything would do!

In desperation, I reminded the doctor, "Sir, you forgot to do the urinalysis." At sixteen, concerned about my father's anger and feeling lousy all the time, I was looking for anything. Something was wrong, and I knew it. The doctor gave me a condescending smile and said, "It won't show anything, but go ahead and leave a sample." I walked to the car feeling awful and wondering what was wrong with me. How could I tell my dad what the doctor had found in the examination? He had determined that I was still just a lazy kid. As we got in the car, a nurse ran out the door of the doctor's office calling, "Mr. Kilmer, you have to come back!" Yes! They had found something! I doubt that anyone in the world has ever been so happy to learn they were seriously ill!

I was going to live! Forget the facts—sure, I would have to take shots and be careful about what I ate for the rest of my life—but if it were possible for a little medication to help me feel good again, I wouldn't be the lazy, worthless kid in the family. (Just to make sure you understand, I'm writing this from the perspective of a scared sixteen-year-old. My dad would never really have hurt me. He would've been very disappointed in me, but he wouldn't have hurt me.)

That night, my dad and mom took me out for what we called my "Last Supper." When Dad allowed me to order anything I wanted, I could tell he was feeling bad about calling me lazy for the last couple of years. Because I loaded up on food, I'm sure my blood sugar was really high the next day when I entered the hospital.

THE DOCTOR WAS ANGRY, THE NURSE WAS IN TROUBLE, AND I WAS HAPPY!

In 1965, the care of diabetes was not as developed as it is today. Certainly our local hospital with its eight rooms didn't see many diabetic patients. I'm convinced that I was the only patient in the hospital at that time because of all the attention I was getting. The way they taught me to give myself a shot seemed a little ridiculous. After all, sticking a needle in an orange is a little different than sticking a needle in your own body! And the food was awful! They had to be kidding—four slices of white bread at one meal with no butter or jelly? No salt on the meat? I thought they called this "sugar diabetes," but they gave me a big stack of vegetables, of all things! I didn't really like vegetables. Maybe it would be better just to be lazy!

However, things got better after lunch! A nurse who had no experience with diabetes came into my room and asked what I wanted for my afternoon snack. My eyes immediately lit up when she asked, "How about a bowl of ice cream?" At the Kilmer house, ice cream was a staple. We ate it as often as possible with great delight in large quantities. "Are you sure this is okay?" I asked. "Oh, sure. Do you want a big bowl or a little one?" she asked. With absolutely no hesitation I replied, "I'll take the biggest one you've got!"

When the doctor arrived a couple of hours later, he was having a hard time figuring out why I wasn't doing better until he learned about the big bowl of ice cream. I felt sorry for the nurse when he left the room looking for her. I knew she was in big trouble. So ended my opportunities to eat big bowls of ice cream! However, to this day I still like a little bite once in a while, and it still tastes good!

A week later I left the hospital with my sugar count under control and feeling really good for the first time in several years. It's a great thing to feel good!

THERE ARE WORSE THINGS THAN BEING A DIABETIC!

My motto for life is a simple one that comes directly from the Bible:

> This is the day that the Lord has made; let us rejoice and be glad in it.
>
> Psalm 118:24

I refuse to waste a day of my life feeling sorry for myself because I'm a diabetic. The truth is that everyone has some kind of illness or problem. In fact, with modern medications and diabetic education, there is no reason for a diabetic to suffer through life.

We are able to enjoy life when we live above our circumstances, not below them. When I ask people how they're doing, sometimes they say, "Pretty good, under the circumstances." I usually try to look down under a table or desk and ask, "What are you doing down there?" Why not live where God put you, above the circumstances? The circumstances of our lives will never be perfect, but no matter what happens, good or bad, we have the ability to respond positively. Choose to live positively and you'll be amazed how little power the circumstances will have over your life.

An important key for living with any chronic illness is a positive attitude! You have the illness! You will live longer and happier with a great attitude.

Consider the following thoughts about your attitude toward your illness:

- Are you ready to set your mind, as much as possible, on the important issues of life, rather than on your pain?

A joyful heart is good medicine, but a crushed spirit dries up the bones.

Proverbs 17:22

A glad heart makes a cheerful face, but by sorrow of heart the spirit is crushed. .. All the days of the afflicted are evil, but the cheerful of heart has a continual feast.

Proverbs 15:13, 15

- Can you make a conscious effort to smile and be warm around other people?

As in water face reflects face, so the heart of man reflects the man.

Proverbs 27:19

- Are you ready for the challenges that will secure your hope in Christ?

Therefore, preparing your minds for action, and being sober-minded, set your hope fully on the grace that will be brought to you at the revelation of Jesus Christ.

1 Peter 1:13

- Are you ready to let your mind dwell on the love of Christ and the love you have for others? If so, He will give you peace.

And above all these put on love, which binds everything together in perfect harmony. And let the peace of Christ rule in your hearts, to which indeed you were called in one body. And be thankful... And whatever you do, in word or deed, do everything in the name of the Lord Jesus, giving thanks to God the Father through him.

Colossians 3:14-15, 17

4

NOT ME!

For you formed my inward parts; you knitted me together in my mother's womb. I praise you, for I am fearfully and wonderfully made. Wonderful are your works; my soul knows it very well. My frame was not hidden from you, when I was being made in secret, intricately woven in the depths of the earth. Your eyes saw my unformed substance; in your book were written, every one of them, the days that were formed for me, when as yet there was none of them. How precious to me are your thoughts, O God! How vast is the sum of them!

Psalm 139:13-17

Have you ever had one of those unpleasant visits to a doctor with whom you just didn't connect? You know the type. Because the doctor doesn't really know you personally, he is going through the same routine he does with all his patients. But never forget—you are not like everyone else! You are a unique creation of God! Keep Psalm 139 in mind every time your doctor explains the terrible nature of your disease. Learn from him, but always keep in mind the fact that it is God who actually controls the universe! Don't give up on life because someone who doesn't know you or your dreams says you can't accomplish your important goals.

Having started with no knowledge of diabetes and very little testing equipment, I was having problems. I needed more information! Six months after my diagnosis, the local doctor recommended a diabetes specialist in a town not far from us. Always wanting to do the best for their children, my mom and dad packed up the car and we took off. One of those great family outings! What could be better than a road trip to the doctor?

After looking at my file, the doctor began to give me careful, rapid-fire instructions. He must have been talking 100 miles an hour: "Take your shots in your thighs, moving one-half inch farther down your leg for each new shot. Go down the front of your leg first, then move over an inch. Repeat, moving over one inch for each line of shots until you have completed one leg. Then move to the other leg, continuing in straight rows over the entire thigh. You must first pick up your vial of insulin and rotate it end over end twelve times. Then swirl it in your hands thirty times..." He was demonstrating by moving the bottle back and forth between his hands very rapidly.

Time out, Doctor! You're talking to a boy who has a hard time remembering the first part of his homework assignments. You actually want me to remember all these things and do them exactly the same way every time? Would you believe, he really expected me to do exactly what he said. Not a chance in the world! I got the idea I needed to shake up my insulin and make sure I changed the location of each shot. What else do I need to know, Doc? By the way, I am still very careful about rotating the places where I give myself a shot! It's important and I know it. However, I probably have never hit exactly one inch or a straight row.

His next question was: "Well, young man, what are you going to do with your life?"

"I'm going to play college football and be a preacher." I thought that was a pretty good answer considering the fact that I was just starting my senior year of high school. At least I had some idea of what I was going to do. However, he frowned and snarled—not a friendly sound at all!

"I doubt you'll be able to handle taking care of your diabetes while playing football," he replied. He was a little behind on that one: I had already played a season of football since being diagnosed with diabetes. Remember, this was the late sixties, back when there was very little in the way of testing supplies to control diabetes. I understood his concern.

"As far as being a preacher, you'll just have to find another occupation," he said. "There's too much stress in the ministry for a man who has diabetes. You will never be able to last. Just make up your mind right now to find a different occupation." He was very emphatic!

Sure, Doc, whatever you say... Not a chance! It sounded like great advice except for the fact that I had a life to live. After almost fifty years of ministry, I must say that I have enjoyed the opportunities God has given me. After all, where else do you get the opportunity to help hundreds of people take a nap while you speak? Honestly, most of them stay awake. In fact, some of them even listen! I have always enjoyed my work, even though there have been a few minor problems along the way.

I must admit, I gained some good insights from that specialist. But the fact is that I considered myself a healthy young man who happened to have diabetes, not a diabetic who was desperately trying to stay healthy. I was not willing to let anyone tell me I couldn't reach my goals because of one difficult part of my life. I was committed to taking proper care of myself and enjoying life.

When I arrived on the campus of Harding University, the fun really started! After an eleven-hour trip from Alva, Oklahoma to Searcy, Arkansas, I quickly settled into my dorm room. There were going to be three of us in a room designed for two, so because there were no belongings in the room yet, I immediately took the best bed and desk for myself. About the time I got settled in, Vance Cox and David Treadwell entered the room. Vance and Dave were both good athletes who had come to Harding on football scholarships. They had actually been in the room before I arrived. They showed some displeasure with the fact that I had put my stuff on Dave's bed and my books in Vance's desk. Yep, nothing like making a good first impression on the people you're going to live with for the next year!

Dave and Vance were not very happy about sharing their two-person room with a non-scholarship athlete, especially as they were less than impressed by my great physical attributes. They were convinced that at 5'6" tall and weighing in at a powerful 156 pounds, I wouldn't last long. In spite of the looks they gave me, they were too nice to tell me what they were really thinking at the time.

The next morning was our first meeting with the team. We woke up early and got ready for breakfast. At the time, our dorm room was not air-conditioned, and we were not allowed to have a refrigerator in the room. The beef insulin we used in those days spoiled quickly, so I had to keep it in the dorm manager's apartment. I hurried downstairs to his apartment, grabbed my insulin, and headed back to the room. I picked up my insulin syringe, sat on the side of the bed, and started to give myself a shot. It was then that I noticed two very shocked faces looking directly at me. After all, the only way to follow a bad first impression is to make it even worse. Remember, this was the late sixties and the drug scene was in high gear. These guys immediately thought I was on drugs! My quick explanation of diabetes convinced them without a doubt that I didn't belong. I'm pretty sure they were hoping I wouldn't last through the first week.

Isn't life fun? I was ready to get on with life and determined to gain the respect not only of my roommates, but also of the other players on the team. In retrospect, I probably could have figured out a better way to start! It took a few days, but Vance and Dave became great friends of mine, and we all enjoyed playing football at Harding.

If you intend to live successfully with a chronic illness, listen and learn, but never let others tell you that you cannot accomplish your goals. Remember: Think like a healthy, positive person even if you happen to have a serious disease. Make every day count!

5

DO I REALLY KNOW WHAT I'M DOING?

His divine power has granted to us all things that pertain to life and godliness, through the knowledge of him who called us to his own glory and excellence.

2 Peter 1:3

The first year I coached football in Atkins, Arkansas, we were not very good. The head coach had been the assistant coach for one year and then had taken over as the head coach. I was his only assistant, and it was my first coaching experience. To make matters much worse, we had only nineteen players on the team, several of whom had never played football in their lives, and only two that had ever been starters in a football game. By midseason, we had been beaten badly in three games and had actually found two other teams that were worse than we were. So as a small Class A school with a 2-3 record, we traveled twelve miles down the road to play Russellville, Arkansas. Russellville was a much larger school and was rated as the overall number one team in the state of Arkansas. Our nineteen boys went out on the field, and their army came out on the field. They must've had seventy or eighty men dressed out for the ballgame.

In the first quarter, our quarterback was knocked out; he would not return to the game. In the second quarter, our second-team quarterback was knocked out. With nineteen boys on the team, we did not have a third-team quarterback. At that point, panic set in, and even though it was second down we did the only thing we could: we punted the football. To help you visualize the situation, we have nineteen players, two of whom are injured, leaving eleven on the field and six on the sideline. We lined five of the six on the sideline up behind our center to see whether any of them could take a snap without dropping the ball. We had to make this move very quickly because Russellville was driving down the field to score again. (It never took more than a couple of minutes for them to score a touchdown.) On our sideline, amidst all the panic, we found a talented sophomore split end named Dale who was able to handle the snap from center. He immediately became our quarterback!

Sure enough, Russellville scored quickly and kicked off, and we got the ball on about our 20-yard line. The head coach put his arm around Dale and said, "Look at the clock. There are only two minutes left in the half. Go out and run 42 (that was our off-tackle play to the right side) three times in a row and take as much time in the huddle as possible. That way, we won't give Russellville a chance to get the ball back and score again before halftime." Dale took off running to the huddle at about 100 miles an hour; he was excited to be playing quarterback. However, he stopped just outside the huddle, dropped his head, and started walking back to the sideline. We were frantic on the sideline, motioning to him to get back in the huddle. The head coach met him on the field and asked what was wrong. I'll never forget his classic response. He said, "Coach, what's a 42?" As a receiver, he had learned only his routes; he had never understood the entire offense.

It's impossible to play football if you don't know the plays. Unfortunately, all Dale understood were his pass routes. I wonder how many of us who are ill know a little about our illness, but don't understand the whole concept of managing our problems as we look for God's wisdom. You see, knowledge is the beginning point of wisdom. It is absolutely essential for those of us who have a serious long-term disease to make wise decisions based upon knowledge.

Remember, even in your pain and suffering, God has a plan for your life!

> And I am sure of this, that he who began a good work in you will bring it to completion at the day of Jesus Christ.
>
> Philippians 1:6

Learn all you can about your disease and the treatment options. Consult with friends and family and make the wisest choices possible. Then "lift up your eyes to the hills" and let the eternal God of the universe watch over your soul!

> I lift up my eyes to the hills. From where does my help come? My help comes from the Lord, who made heaven and earth. He will not let your foot be moved; he who keeps you will not slumber. Behold, he who keeps Israel will neither slumber nor sleep. The Lord is your keeper; the Lord is your shade on your right hand. The sun will not strike you by day, nor the moon by night. The Lord will keep you from all evil; he will

keep your life. The Lord will keep your going out and your coming in from this time forth and forevermore.

Psalm 121

Don't just learn about your illness; learn about unique opportunities that you may have to encourage and strengthen other people! It is never fun to be in pain, but the pain is lifted when you focus on other people. The more you help others, the more you see God's Holy Spirit working in your life. The more we extend our thoughts outside our pain, the less we notice the pain. It is mind over matter—focusing all your thoughts on something meaningful until you almost don't notice the pain.

> For this reason I bow my knees before the Father, from whom every family in heaven and on earth is named, that according to the riches of his glory he may grant you to be strengthened with power through his Spirit in your inner being, so that Christ may dwell in your hearts through faith—that you, being rooted and grounded in love, may have strength to comprehend with all the saints what is the breadth and length and height and depth, and to know the love of Christ that surpasses knowledge, that you may be filled with all the fullness of God. Now to him who is able to do far more abundantly than all that we ask or think, according to

the power at work within us, to him be glory in the church and in Christ Jesus throughout all generations, forever and ever. Amen.

Ephesians 3:14-21

The sufferings we have today are nothing compared with the joy that the Holy Spirit gives to us. God uses His presence in our life to lift us above the circumstances of our pain and illness so we can see His glory. In the eighth chapter of Romans, Paul shares with us the power of allowing the Spirit to control our hearts:

> For I consider that the sufferings of this present time are not worth comparing with the glory that is to be revealed to us.
>
> Romans 8:18

Continue reading a few verses later and see the power God gives us in our weakness:

> Likewise the Spirit helps us in our weakness. For we do not know what to pray for as we ought, but the Spirit himself intercedes for us with groanings too deep for words. And he who searches hearts knows what is the mind of the Spirit, because the Spirit intercedes for

the saints according to the will of God. And we know that for those who love God all things work together for good, for those who are called according to his purpose.

Romans 8:26-28

Take a few moments to consider the following thoughts:

- How much have you learned about your illness since you first became sick?

- During that time, how much have you learned about God's ultimate plan for your life?

- Look deeply into your heart and see what God has placed there for you to accomplish.

- Consider what you were doing the last time you didn't notice your pain as much.

- What can you do to glorify God that will take your thoughts off your illness?

PART 2:

TRUE STORIES OF SOARING ABOVE SUFFERING

6

NINETY-THREE YEARS OLD, SMILING & HAPPY

THE STORY OF DURCIE TURNER

I thank my God in all my remembrance of you, always in every prayer of mine for you all making my prayer with joy, because of your partnership in the gospel from the first day until now. And I am sure of this, that he who began a good work in you will bring it to completion at the day of Jesus Christ.

Philippians 1:3-6

And above all these put on love, which binds everything together in perfect harmony. And let the peace of Christ rule in your hearts, to which indeed you were called in one body. And be thankful.

Colossians 3:14-15

No one has had a greater impact on my life than Durcie Turner.

As surprising as it may sound, some of my greatest heroes are elderly widows. Durcie Turner is one of my all-time great heroes. No, she did not have diabetes; she had something worse: terminal cancer. At the age of 86, she had been told that she had only a short time to live. On a warm August day, I stopped to talk with her while she mowed the yard of her little home, which was right behind the church where I preached. At age 93, Durcie was still alive and active. She had the most beautiful, toothless smile I've ever seen. She loved to work in the yard and grow vegetables in her garden, giving them freely to her friends and neighbors. This cheerful, pleasant little lady who had been fighting cancer for almost six years never complained about her health problems. She had a contagiously positive attitude that had a great impact on my life.

Not long after her ninety-third birthday, the cancer got the best of Durcie, and she was forced into the hospital. Picture her lying in her hospital bed, an 86-pound, 93-year-old lady who was in pain every minute of every day, alone and waiting to die. She had every reason to be bitter and unhappy, yet she had a cheerful spirit and a warm smile. Her wonderful attitude was always inspiring to me, so I would wait until I was a little discouraged to go see her.

The only thing Durcie didn't like was a nursing home. Some stories she had heard about nursing homes scared her, and she never wanted to live in one. Her goal was either to go home and finish harvesting her garden or to go to her real home with Jesus in heaven, where she would be safe with the Lord. The only place in the world she did not want to be was in a nursing home. She begged the doctors, "Please don't send me to one of those places!"

However, things got worse for Durcie when the doctors realized there was nothing more they could do for her in the hospital; the only place for her now was a nursing home. I have to admit, I hesitated before going to see her for the first time in that awful place. Nursing homes were not nearly as well controlled back then as they are now. I remember the sterile appearance, the nursing-home smell, and the big metal door. This just didn't seem to be the right place for a sweet little lady. She now weighed 84 pounds, couldn't get out of bed, was in constant pain, and was living in the one place in all the world where she did not want to be. I paused outside her room, not wanting to see Durcie's suffering. After some hesitation, I opened the door and walked in.

I immediately heard Durcie's excited voice coming from the second bed in the room: "Dean, come over here! I've got something to tell you!" I walked to her bedside, looked at that wonderful toothless smile, and asked, "Durcie, what are you so excited about?" She pointed to the bed next to her and remarked, "That's JoAnne, and she's the reason God put me here!" What an incredible spirit! She went on to explain that JoAnne had suffered a stroke, which had caused her to lose the use of her body except for one arm and one leg. Sometimes at night, JoAnne would get cold because she had kicked the covers off the bed with her good leg. At other times when she was hurting, she would wave her arm in pain. Durcie was always on the lookout! Although she couldn't get out of bed to help, she could hit the call button to let the nurses know that JoAnne was having trouble. It was now her mission in life to take care of JoAnne! With that mission and a call button, she drove the nurses crazy!

At age 93, and at the point of death from a disease worse than most of us have, this wonderful lady was experiencing the joy of living to help someone else. She knew God had put her on this earth for a purpose, and she found great joy in fulfilling her purpose. I am confident that Durcie had no idea of the number of lives she would touch. However, I have used her example in seminars, sermons, workshops, Bible classes, and books for the past 30 years. I also know of other preachers who have used her example in their lessons. I'm convinced that hundreds and maybe thousands of people have been influenced by the faith of a 93-year-old lady who had cancer. If God could use her in such a powerful way, what can He do with your life and example?

TO FIND JOY IN LIFE, LIVE FOR A HIGHER PURPOSE! YOU WILL BE HEALTHIER AND STRONGER.

I have been in several hospitals for the mentally ill—No, not as a patient!—visiting people who were struggling with depression or even more challenging mental-health issues. There is one similarity among all those I have visited who battled serious mental problems. This overwhelming similarity cannot be ignored or overlooked. What is this powerful problem that every one of these patients exhibits? They are always talking about themselves! The comments are always, "What is wrong with me?" "Why don't people like me?" "Why can't I get my life straightened out?" "I'm just an awful person." Those and hundreds of similar comments are repeated over and over by individuals with emotional struggles. They are feeling bad about themselves and are afraid that others look down on them. The whole world centers on their view of themselves. The best cure for sadness or depression is to look outside yourself and help other people. I know you are sick and hurting! I understand the all-consuming nature of chronic illness. However, the more it consumes us, the more it controls us! When we help someone else, we lift them up and at the same time lift ourselves up. Developing peace of mind and a cheerful heart is a challenging project because the more we direct our thoughts to ourselves, the more we worry about ourselves. Peace and joy are built by developing a higher purpose. When we realize our opportunities to help other people, our focus changes as we see the light in their eyes. Our own eyes light up and peace of mind overtakes our frustrations when another person's eyes shine with delight!

Your illness may be harsh and rapidly advancing, but there are two things that will lift you above your present suffering. The first is loving other people. You have family members who love you, and you can leave them a legacy of love through your great faith, courage, and joy. When they see you facing your illness and still smiling and blessing their lives with laughter, they will forever be thankful.

The second and more important element that lifts us above our present suffering is our love for God. The suffering of this life is only short-term, but the reality of a life in heaven is eternal. The love of our Savior is always evident in the cross.

If you look, you will find God's purpose in life! Somehow, some way, God will use you if you let Him. Mark the ways God can use you this week:

- Respond warmly to those who call you on the phone.
- Give a smile to every visitor who comes to see you.
- Ask questions about your visitors' families and show concern. Pray for their family members.
- As they pray for you, verbally pray for them as well.
- Ask your family and friends to sing praises to God with you.
- If you are unable to attend worship, invite others to your house to worship God as you view a DVD of worship services at your church.

- Be sure to invite those who normally don't worship God. Your faith will have an impact on their souls.

7

A SOUL THIRSTY FOR GOD

THE STORY OF GENE CAMPBELL

Praise the Lord! Sing to the Lord a new song, his praise in the assembly of the godly!

Psalm 149:1

Praise the Lord! Praise the Lord from the heavens; praise him in the heights! Praise him, all his angels; praise him, all his hosts! Praise him, sun and moon, praise him, all you shining stars! Praise him, you highest heavens, and you waters above the heavens!

Psalm 148:1-4

Nothing lifts the heart more than joyful singing! If you are a singer or you enjoy listening to great uplifting songs, let God

SOARING ABOVE THE CIRCUMSTANCES

lift your heart as you experience His joy in praise.

Gene Campbell was a dedicated Christian who loved to lead singing and worship the Lord. He was heavily involved in a gospel singing group called So Noted, which performed at many of our church gatherings and other activities. His outstanding singing voice and his pleasant demeanor made him a natural at inspiring people through his singing. He also served as an elder for the church of Christ in Waxahachie, Texas. As an elder he was a strong leader with a good understanding of the Bible and the courage to stand up for the truth.

He was a leader for his family, including his children and grandchildren. His love for all of them was obvious. Gene and Loyce shared their love for God with their family through their love for singing, using their natural talents to raise their children to love the Lord.

When the doctors first told Gene about his cancer, it was quite a shock! However, it got even worse for Gene when the doctor said it was a fast-growing cancer. The questions then began: How long do I have? What is the best treatment? How will I feel during the treatment? Will I be able to enjoy any good days? For Gene all the answers were challenging. He had a fast-growing cancer, the treatment would be painful, and it would not allow him to live much longer. What do you do with such a dreadful diagnosis?

For Gene the decision was natural: He continued to serve God as he always had. He worshiped with us at the Brown Street Church of Christ as long as his strength allowed. He even served on the building committee, which helped plan our new building. When the cancer became so severe that he could no longer leave his home, Gene and Loyce continued to worship God.

Every Sunday morning at exactly the time of our worship services, Gene and Loyce would move to the living room, put on the DVD of the previous week's worship, take out the fruit of the vine and the loaf for the communion and worship with the church from their home. This home worship continued for several months until Gene was unable to get out of his bed.

During those last couple of months, they moved the DVD player into the bedroom, and Gene's children and grandchildren gathered around him as he worshiped from his bed. As the congregation sang on the DVD, they joined in the singing from his bedroom. When the congregation observed the Lord's Supper, they celebrated the death, burial and resurrection of Christ together around his bed.

I believe that during those few weeks, the most inspiring worship that took place in our congregation was there in that bedroom as Gene helped his family draw closer to God. While many people give up on life when they become critically ill, Gene became an even greater example for his family and for all of us who knew him. What remarkable faith! What impressive strength! What a marvelous example! What can you do when you're critically ill? You can strengthen the faith of your family and other people! Inspire others as you continuously give your heart to God.

> As a deer pants for flowing streams, so pants my soul for you, O God. My soul thirsts for God, for the living God. When shall I come and appear before God?
>
> Psalm 42:1-2

LIFT YOUR VOICE, YOUR HEART, AND YOUR SOUL TO GOD, AND HE WILL UPLIFT YOU!

You'll be amazed how much better your days can be if you open your heart to God and let a song of praise come into your soul. Consider the following ways you can allow God to lift your heart this week:

- Sing a song of praise as soon as you wake up in the morning. Follow your song with a prayer of sincere thanksgiving for all your blessings.

- Listen to gospel music on a Christian radio station or CD. Sing along as you listen.

- If you're not a good singer, whistle a Christian song.

- Read the songs in a good songbook and meditate on the uplifting words.

8

WHAT DO YOU DO WHEN YOUR WORLD IS TURNED UPSIDE-DOWN?

BY ROBIN PHILLIPS

> Humble yourselves, therefore, under the mighty hand of God so that at the proper time he may exalt you, casting all your anxieties upon him, because he cares for you.
>
> 1 Peter 5:6-7

The last Sunday in January of 2010 started out like any other Sunday morning for our family. I woke up, made hot tea for myself and coffee for Steve, my husband of 35 years, and sat down to read my devotional while sipping tea. Then I brought the newspaper in and started Sunday lunch. At 7:30, I took Steve his coffee and paper. We visited about the day ahead and made plans. As I was getting ready to go to church, Steve said he thought he was coming down with a stomach bug. He encouraged me to go on to church, saying he would be fine. While I was in class, my phone lit up, and I returned the call. I was asked to come home; there was an emergency. As I approached our home, I saw the emergency vehicles. Paramedics were working with Steve. Soon they rushed him to the hospital. After 36 hours, our three beautiful children and I said our goodbyes to a wonderful husband and the best "hands-on" dad any children could have. Steve, age 57, had died from a virus that had attacked his heart. We knew that he had gone to be with our Lord in eternity. He loved God and was a faithful servant.

We were able to get through the next few days because we were so blessed to have family, church family, and friends supporting us ... holding us before the Lord. The immediate loneliness was overwhelming. During that time, I quietly reflected on the poem "Footprints." I knew the only reason we were still upright was because God is faithful. He was holding us up and guiding us through.

Steve was a businessman who owned two companies. He had approximately fifty employees. Both of our sons, our niece, and I were among those fifty. After working for six months and trying to keep the business going, we had to shut down. By this time, most of the employees had found other jobs; there were only six employees remaining. We were all without jobs and insurance. In 1 Peter 5:6-7, I read, "Humble yourselves, therefore, under the mighty hand of God, that he may exalt you at the proper time, casting all your anxiety upon him, because he cares for you."

IT WAS HARD TO BELIEVE, BUT THINGS ACTUALLY GOT WORSE!

After three weeks of searching for a job, I was finally granted an interview. On the same day, as Steve's executrix, I was served with papers of a lawsuit against both companies and his estate for the debt that came due upon the owner's death. When it seems God's hand may not be upon you, it is. I got the job. My emotions were so mixed: I wondered how I was to handle a new job and appear in court for the hearings. One night, as I felt Satan pulling, filling me with doubts, I read James 1:2-4: "Consider it pure joy, my brothers, whenever you face trials of many kinds, because you know that the testing of your faith develops perseverance. Perseverance must finish its work so that you may be mature and complete, not lacking anything. "

With God's help and the encouragement and prayer of family and friends, all of us had jobs within six months. I stayed in that position for four years. My employer was very understanding and gracious, allowing me to make the court appearances. And in return, I was able to honor them by making up my time at lunch, staying late, and working on Saturdays.

The company sold, and the new owners required me to travel at least once a month. I began to seek another job, hoping to land a bookkeeping position that would not require travel. After several months, some friends asked me to give them my resume so they could pray over it. After three weeks, two friends called and said they had forwarded my resume on to a friend of ours. I was told that she was sending the resume to someone she knew and that if I received a phone call from a certain company, I should be sure to talk to them. I could feel God at work in my life. Jesus says in Matthew 7:7-8, "Ask, and it shall be given to you; seek, and you shall find; knock, and it shall be opened to you. For everyone who asks receives, and he who seeks finds, and to him who knocks it shall be opened." After a phone call and three interviews, I was offered a position in the accounting department. Yes, it was a bookkeeping job! I was working in a company with people who believed in God, and the atmosphere at work was so uplifting.

WHEN WE ARE AT OUR WEAKEST POINT, GOD DEMONSTRATES HIS STRENGTH AND LOVE!

Four months after starting in the accounting office, I fell at work, crushed a bone in my leg, and spent the next three weeks in the hospital and rehabilitation. The surgeon explained that I would not be able to put any weight on my left leg for three months. Immediately I felt anxious about everything. (Ever feel like Job???) As I lay in bed waiting for the surgery, a friend sent a card to me at the hospital. At the bottom, she wrote Matthew 6:34: "Therefore do not be anxious for tomorrow; for tomorrow will care for itself. Each day has enough trouble of its own." I started focusing my prayers, not only on healing, but on the care of my children and my grandson. I asked God to reveal my purpose in life and how I could serve Him.

The healing process has taken longer than anticipated. It required a second surgery. Immediately after the second surgery, I was back in therapy and finally making progress.

What a blessing! My employer had been so gracious, holding my position longer than was required. However, the time came that my position had to be filled, which caused me to lose health insurance benefits. But even in trials we are blessed! My church family came together and furnished the means to cover several months of insurance for us. I was so grateful and overwhelmed by the love shown to me. We are told in Romans 8:28, "And we know that God causes all things to work together for good to those who love God, to those who are called according to His purpose."

In answer to the question posed in the title of this chapter, when you feel your world has turned upside-down, all you can do is have faith in God, stay in God's Word, and be constant in prayer. You have to count the many blessings and joys you have in your life, remembering a faithful God who cares for His own.

LIVE EACH DAY TO THE GLORY OF GOD, AND HE WILL TAKE CARE OF YOU!

When I read Robin's story, I am inspired to consider the closeness of my relationship with God. I have to confess, I usually don't spend much time in meditation until I'm pressed into a corner. When your world is collapsing all around you, take time to mediate on some of these passages:

> Now to him who is able to do far more abundantly than all that we ask or think according to the power at work within us, to him be glory in the church and in Christ Jesus throughout all generations, forever and ever. Amen.
>
> Ephesians 3:20-21

Take a deep breath and let God's strength dwell in your mind and heart.

> Peace I leave with you; my peace I give to you. Not as the world gives do I give to you. Let not your hearts be troubled, neither let them be afraid.
>
> John 14:27

Fear drives our stress to unbearable heights, but faith replaces it with God's promised peace.

> This Book of the Law shall not depart from your mouth, but you shall meditate on it day and night, so that you may be careful to do according to all that is written in it. For then you will make your way prosperous, and then

you will have good success. Have I not commanded you? Be strong and courageous. Do not be frightened, and do not be dismayed, for the Lord your God is with you wherever you go.

Joshua 1:8-9

Courage and peace come directly from God.

9

THE SERENDIPITY OF SUFFERING

BY PAUL O'REAR

Count it all joy, my brothers, when you meet trials of various kinds, for you know that the testing of your faith produces steadfastness. And let steadfastness have its full effect, that you may be perfect and complete, lacking in nothing.

James 1:2-4

For the past sixteen years or so, I have suffered from a condition called peripheral neuropathy, apparently resulting from a one-time vitamin B12 deficiency that caused deterioration of the nerve sheathings in my feet, which caused the nerves in my feet to die. Basically, I have no feeling in my feet. Besides just being weird, this has created a series of other problems.

If I get a blister on the bottom of my foot, it will likely turn into a sore that will gradually get bigger and deeper and will take a long time—like, a really long time—to heal. The worst sore I ever had ended up being about two to two-and-a-half inches in diameter, right on the ball of my foot, and remained an open wound for about two years before it finally healed. Strangely, that sore never became infected. Others have.

One sore became so seriously infected that I had to have the little toe on my left foot amputated. It looked like a shark had taken a bite out of my foot! My wife, Susan, took pictures of it. (She's weird like that.)

Another serious sore resulted in a staph infection that got into my bloodstream and started spreading throughout my body. That one landed me in the hospital for over a week, followed by eight weeks of at-home intravenous antibiotics (two of the strongest ones available). But the infection did not kill me. I consider that a good thing.

Because of the neuropathy, I developed a related condition in both feet known as Charcot foot. Charcot causes the bones in the foot to collapse and even fracture, resulting in moderate to severe deformity of the foot and instability of the foot's infrastructure, creating an increased potential for sores. Both of my feet required bone reconstruction surgery, at different times, in an attempt to return the bones to a semi-normal, stable condition.

My first botched foot surgery caused the big toe on my right foot to turn sideways. A later successful surgery on that same foot finally straightened out my toe (mostly), making it possible for me to wear regular shoes again.

Another botched surgery on my other foot, several years later, left me with a dropped bone in the bottom middle of my left foot (where most people have an arch), creating a constant pressure point that put me at risk of yet another sore. I went to an orthotics doctor who custom-built a brace that cradled the protrusion and kept it from rubbing a sore. That worked great for a while, until the brace rubbed a callous on the ball of my foot that eventually turned into another nasty sore that landed me back in the hospital.

It would be impossible to estimate the amount of time I have spent on crutches, in wheelchairs, on knee walkers and motorized scooters, wearing specialized shoes and casts and boots and braces, and using a walker to get around (the kind you see people using in nursing homes); or to calculate the loss of personal and professional productivity created by such reductions in mobility.

Oh, and the whole dead-nerves-resulting-in-no-feeling thing—it has been gradually spreading to my hands over the past few years. I now have very little feeling in my fingers, which makes a lot of everyday tasks increasingly difficult: buckling a belt, tying my shoes, buttoning a shirt, putting on a necktie, playing a guitar or ukulele, using a fork and knife, writing, signing my name, and typing (a frustrating problem for a writer), to name just a few.

To complicate matters, I also suffer from severe gout, which has presented itself at various times in nearly every joint of my body. Gout is extremely painful and debilitating. When it attacks a knee, it can make walking exceedingly difficult. When it flares up in an elbow, shoulder, or hand, it can render that entire arm useless. Even picking up light objects becomes nearly impossible.

The most recent gout attack lasted about three months, moving between my shoulders, elbows, wrists, and fingers, with constant pain in some part of my upper body for the entire three-month period. This was during a time that I was supposed to be non-weight-bearing because of a sore on my foot. The gout made it impossible to use crutches.

SERENDIPITY

So why would I title this chapter "The Serendipity of Suffering"? The word *serendipity* means "an unexpected blessing." I believe suffering has the potential to bring with it some unexpected blessings, if only we are willing to see them and recognize them as such. Let me share two of those blessings with you.

WHO IS IN CONTROL?

First, my suffering reminds me that I am not in control. God is. It certainly was not in my plans to spend the last decade and a half of my life in and out of wheelchairs and hospitals, becoming less and less independent because of the things that are becoming more and more difficult to do. Those circumstances were conspicuously absent from any game plan I had crafted for my life.

But my plans do not really matter. Those frustrating circumstances are here, whether I want them or not, whether I planned for them or not. I am not in control.

God's plans for my life are the ones that count. The things that you and I want for our lives might not fit with His plans, and they might even be counterproductive. I must be willing to submit my will to His, even if His will includes my suffering. I have believed for a long time that God can sometimes accomplish more through us in our suffering than in our comfort. I don't like that, but I believe it is the truth.

It was not my plan to spend the last sixteen years suffering. But I am convinced that it was (and apparently still is) God's plan for me to suffer. How do I know that? It is actually quite simple.

I have prayed countless times for God to heal my foot problems and allow me to spend the rest of my days being able to get up in the mornings and put on my shoes and walk, just like normal people do. Countless times. And I believe that this is a perfectly reasonable request. It is certainly within the scope of His power to grant such a request. Fix a couple of messed-up feet? No problem for God. And yet His answer, time and again, has obviously been, "No."

Why would God not grant my request? I do not know the answer to that question, except that it is apparent that He has a plan for my suffering. I don't know what that plan is; and, quite frankly, I don't like that plan, whatever it is. But I am not in control. And that is a powerful reality that I need to be reminded of. Suffering reminds me.

COUNTING BLESSINGS

Second, my suffering reminds me that I need to count my blessings. "I complained because I had no shoes, until I met a man who had no feet."

No matter how bad your situation is, it could always be worse. At the beginning of this chapter, I spent considerable verbiage recounting some of the details of my sixteen years of suffering. It may have sounded like a pity party. It was not. Let me explain.

I don't want you to feel sorry for me because there is no reason to do so. As frustrating and annoying and maddening as my problems are, I remind myself every day that they could be a lot worse. For some people, they are a lot worse.

There are numerous diabetics whose doctors start removing body parts instead of patching them when they start having foot problems similar to mine. They end up stuck in wheelchairs for the rest of their lives with no legs or feet. I have a lot to be thankful for.

Countless young men and women selflessly go to some of the most God-forsaken places on earth to fight for my freedom and yours. Many of them come back with physical and emotional scars that will haunt them for the rest of their lives. Many of them do not come back at all. I have a lot to be thankful for.

Many people suffer from diseases and ailments that make my foot problems seem trivial.

Radiation and chemotherapy treatments wreak utter havoc on the bodies of cancer patients, many of whom are children.

Severe depression can steal every ounce of joy from a person's life and make life miserable and unbearable.

Diabetes is the ninth-leading cause of death in the world and can result in blindness, amputations, stroke, and heart disease.

I have a lot to be thankful for!

THE TAKE-AWAY

I described my suffering in some detail so that you would understand that I am not talking theory here. I am writing from sixteen years in the trenches. I am accustomed to changing my plans, and even the very course of my life, to accommodate my infirmities. I know the frustration of realizing that there are some things that I can no longer do, and will never again be able to do, because of my stinkin' feet, and now because of my hands as well.

So what's the take-away message from all of this? It is really pretty simple.

No matter what happens in this life, God is still the one in control. I must submit my will to His. And if His will for my life includes suffering, then so be it.

Even on my worst day, there are many people who would trade places with me in a heartbeat because my "suffering" is a walk in the park compared to theirs.

So it makes no sense to feel sorry for myself (though I admit that I sometimes do) nor to seek pity from others. My situation could be a whole lot worse than it is, and so I simply count my blessings.

And my blessings are numerous!

And in a sense, suffering is actually one of those blessings.

Not only that, but we rejoice in our sufferings, knowing that suffering produces endurance, and endurance produces character, and character produces hope, and hope does not put us to shame, because God's love has been poured into our hearts through the Holy Spirit who has been given to us.

Romans 5:3-5

10

THE DOCTOR REFUSED TO LOOK HER IN THE EYE

THE STORY OF ANNE FORD

And who knows whether you have not come to the kingdom for such a time as this?

Esther 4:14

We live expecting everything to be perfect in our lives, and then God rearranges our plans. How could God possibly take Anne Ford and her husband, Tom, in a new and extremely challenging direction and still give them peace and comfort? It is amazing to see the strength that our God has provided for Anne in exactly the way he describes in 2 Corinthians 1:2. When Anne first found the sore on the roof of her mouth, it seemed so insignificant. However, the dentist referred her to another doctor. After an examination, without ever looking her in the face, the doctor told her she had cancer, she would never eat another sandwich, and she would need surgery, which would disfigure her.

It seemed to Anne as if an execution had taken place. The doctor had refused to give her any hope for the future, and he hadn't even had the courage to look at her when he spoke.

When Anne shared the news with her family, they agreed to look for a doctor who would treat her with compassion. At MD Anderson Hospital in Houston, they were able to find a doctor who gave them some hope. The trip through her cancer would be hard, the treatment would be disfiguring, but her life was not over. Fourteen years after her first surgery, Anne is a tremendous inspiration to everyone who knows her! She is unable to eat solid food, and the results of her surgery are apparent. Since that first surgery, she has experienced four additional surgeries, including a stem cell transplant. In all those years with all the hardships and surgeries, she has never become angry with God, nor has she ever doubted that He has a purpose for her life.

It's always amazing when we plan our lives expecting everything to turn out exactly the way we want and suddenly

God's plan changes everything. When Anne's life didn't go the way she had expected, she learned the blessing of God's complete comfort.

COMFORT THROUGH THE PRAYERS OF MANY

> You also must help us by prayer, so that many will give thanks on our behalf for the blessing granted us through the prayers of many.
>
> 2 Corinthians 1:11

John Schadegg, the minister of the 60-member Northwest Church of Christ in Lincoln, Nebraska, organized a 24-hour prayer chain on the day that Anne faced her first 15-hour surgery. Knowing that the prayers were continuously being offered on her behalf around the clock gave her the strength to go through that first frightening facial surgery. She remarked, "I could feel the prayers being offered!" It was God's power working through the many people praying for her!

COMFORT FROM CHRIST

With all the prayers and support, Anne came through the

surgery with flying colors. The only problem was that it didn't work! They had taken part of a bone from her leg to replace her cheek bone, and in a few days her reconstructed cheek collapsed. Seven days later, she was in surgery again. Was it now time to give up? No, it was only time to look deeper into God's love and mercy.

> Blessed be the God and Father of our Lord Jesus Christ, the Father of mercies and God of all comfort, who comforts us in all our affliction, so that we may be able to comfort those who are in any affliction, with the comfort with which we ourselves are comforted by God.
>
> 2 Corinthians 1:3-4

Yes, there is a purpose in God's plan: He gives us comfort and strength for every challenge so that we in turn can comfort others. Anne Ford took God's comfort and became a guiding light by helping to start a pillow ministry for those in the hospital. Every month, 300 pillows are made by our ladies at the Brown Street Church of Christ and sent to Lifeline Chaplaincy, who gives them to surgical patients in Dallas hospitals. Cancer and all, Anne uses God's comfort to comfort others.

COMFORT BY SHARING SUFFERING WITH OTHERS

Anne was determined to share her faith with others, to be a blessing in the lives of others who suffered, and it was that determination that gave her comfort in her own hardships—exactly as Paul had said it would.

> If we are afflicted, it is for your comfort and salvation; and if we are comforted, it is for your comfort, which you experience when you patiently endure the same sufferings that we suffer. Our hope for you is unshaken, for we know that as you share in our sufferings, you will also share in our comfort.
>
> 2 Corinthians 1:6-7

Powerful bonds form when Christians share their faith during their suffering, lifting one another up in the love of Christ. Tom shared in Anne's suffering. As you know, caregivers always suffer side by side with their loved ones. Tom's strength lifted Anne up when she faced another unkind doctor before her stem cell transplant. When she talked about the help her husband gave her, the doctor bluntly said, "I'm surprised he's still around." She hadn't got over the shock of that hateful remark when the doctor said, "You brought this cancer on yourself." Again shocked by his statement, she asked for an explanation, but he refused to explain himself and walked out of the room. The uncaring doctor didn't understand her faith or Tom's.

Anne spent twenty days isolated in a small hospital room recovering slowly from the complete destruction of her immune system and from her doctor's harsh, unfeeling words. Surprise!—she recovered faster than any other patient in the entire treatment center! It's amazing what God does when His people share their suffering and their faith with others who love them.

GOD WILL DELIVER US FROM THE PERIL OF DEATH!

> Indeed, we felt that we had received the sentence of death. But that was to make us rely not on ourselves but on God who raises the dead. He delivered us from such a deadly peril, and he will deliver us. On him we have set our hope that he will deliver us again.
>
> 2 Corinthians 1:9-10

Delivered from death by God for fourteen years now, Anne Ford is an inspiration to her children and grandchildren and to her church family, who see the light of Christ in her. Her goal every day is to "stay engaged" in life by helping other people. Anne spends more time thinking about others than about her desire to be healed. She has taken strength from the prayers of others.

A great way to stay engaged in life would be to spend a month praying the prayers of the apostle Paul. When we read his prayers in the Bible, we find that he prayed only once for healing; his other prayers were for the spiritual growth of the people he loved. Take this month and pray for the following things.

- Pray that those you love will have their hearts enlightened with the Spirit of wisdom and hope.

I do not cease to give thanks for you, remembering you in my prayers, that the God of our Lord Jesus Christ, the Father of glory, may give you the Spirit of wisdom and of revelation in the knowledge of him, having the eyes of your hearts enlightened, that you may know what is the hope to which he has called you, what are the riches of his glorious inheritance in the saints.

Ephesians 1:16-18

- Pray that the Holy Spirit will give you strength, enabling you to understand the depth of God's love.

For this reason I bow my knees before the Father, from whom every family in heaven and on earth is named, that according to the riches of his glory he may grant you to be strengthened with power through his Spirit in your inner being, so that Christ may dwell in your hearts through faith—that you, being rooted and grounded in love, may have strength to comprehend with all the saints what is the breadth and length and height and depth, and to know the love of Christ that surpasses knowledge, that you may be filled with all the fullness of God. Now to him who is able to do far more abundantly than all that we ask or think, according to the power at work within us, to him be glory in the church and in Christ Jesus throughout all generations, forever and ever. Amen.

Ephesians 3:14-21

- Pray that those you love might abound more and more in love. Pray that they will learn how to love with knowledge and discernment as they live pure lives in Christ.

And it is my prayer that your love may abound more and more, with knowledge and all discernment, so that you may approve what is excellent, and so be pure and blameless for the day of Christ, filled with the fruit of righteousness that comes through Jesus Christ, to the glory and praise of God.

Philippians 1:9-11

- Pray for spiritual wisdom, so that those you love will walk in a manner pleasing to the Lord and bring forth fruit from their good works.

And so, from the day we heard, we have not ceased to pray for you, asking that you may be filled with the knowledge of his will in all spiritual wisdom and understanding, so as to walk in a manner worthy of the Lord, fully pleasing to him, bearing fruit in every good work and increasing in the knowledge of God. May you be strengthened with all power, according to his glorious might, for all endurance and patience with joy.

Colossians 1:9-11

11

A GOOD HEART AND AN UNEXPECTED BLESSING

THE STORY OF BILLY PERRYMAN

> I waited patiently for the Lord; he inclined to me and heard my cry. He drew me up in the pit of destruction, out of my miry bog, and set my feet upon a rock, making my steps secure. He put a new song in my mouth, a song of praise to our God. Many will see and fear, and put their trust in the Lord.
>
> Psalm 40:1-3

Glen and Connie Perryman were devastated when the doctor explained their young son's condition. Billy was going to live, but he had multiple sclerosis (MS). The consequences of the disease would be a challenge for the rest of his life. At that moment, Glen and Connie came to a couple of very important conclusions. First, they realized this was not the end. Their son, Billy, was alive, and even though his quality of life would never be what they had hoped for, he could still have a meaningful life. Secondly, they realized that he was God's child. Whatever else might happen in his life, he belonged to God first.

Billy is a grown man now. Because of his illness, he is unable to hold a regular job and is often subject to seizures and other health problems. However, Glen and Connie have good reason to be very proud of their son. Billy's life is different from other people's lives, but his life glorifies God every day. While Billy was still in school, the Perrymans were called in to a conference with his teacher. Instead of telling them that Billy was in trouble and always behind in his work, the teacher said she wished all of her students were like Billy. It seems there was a disabled boy who never mingled with the other children and sat at a table all by himself in his wheelchair during lunch. Noticing the boy, Billy went over and pushed his wheelchair to a table where he could eat with the other children. From that day forward, the boy sat at their table and Billy helped wheel him around the school. What a blessing Billy was! God had used him to bless the life of a disabled child.

As an adult, Billy has continued to bless people's lives. Justin had just been released from prison, where he had served time for manslaughter. He was driving home when he ran out of gas. Going to a gas station, he decided to ask someone for only two dollars to buy enough gas to go home. Having just been released from prison, he was afraid no one would help him. It took all the nerve he could muster to ask the first person he met for a handout of two dollars. When he asked, he was surprised by the response. The man gave him a twenty-dollar bill and said, "God bless you."

Several years later, Billy was helping his father in a Celebrate Recovery program when a man walked in and told the story of how his life was changed the night after he was released from prison. He ran out of gas and had no money on him. He headed toward a gas station, afraid that no one would be willing to help an ex-con. He explained that he asked the first man he saw for two dollars so that he could get home. He stated, "That kind man gave me a twenty dollar bill and said, 'God bless you.' Those words made me realize that blessing comes from God." He pointed across the room directly at Billy and said, "That man changed my life!" He was now in a class learning about God and planning to become a Christian. God had planted Billy in just the right place with just the right spirit to help change Justin's eternal destiny.

Consider the questions below:

- Have you allowed your life to bless others since you have become ill?

- When have you been able to bless someone's life in a small way?

- Have you ever said, "God bless you"?

- Have you looked deeply into the hearts of people around you to see their emotions?

- Are you planning to become the strongest person among all who suffer from your illness?

- Have you counted your blessings today?

PART 3:

BIBLICAL POWER TO SOAR ABOVE YOUR STRUGGLES

12

STRENGTH WHEN YOUR PRAYERS ARE NOT ANSWERED

So to keep me from becoming conceited because of the surpassing greatness of the revelations, a thorn was given me in the flesh, a messenger of Satan to harass me, to keep me from becoming conceited. Three times I pleaded with the Lord about this, that it should leave me. But he said to me, "My grace is sufficient for you, for my power is made perfect in weakness." Therefore I will boast all the more gladly of my weaknesses, so that the power of Christ may rest upon me. For the sake of Christ, then, I am content with weaknesses, insults, hardships, persecutions, and calamities. For when I am weak, then I am strong.

2 Corinthians 12:7-10

When I look back on my life, I have known many great, faithful Christians who have been healed of devastating diseases by God's power in answer to their prayers. However, I've also known many dedicated, strong, faithful Christians who pray, just as earnestly with just as much faith, and yet have not been healed.

WHY HAS GOD HEALED ONE AND NOT THE OTHER?

The answer is found in God's marvelous, eternal plan to give light to the world. Paul had complete faith in the power of God to heal him. However, after his multiple requests for healing were denied, it became obvious what God had planned for his life. Evidently God knew that His light could be seen more clearly through Paul if he were weak! What a challenging thought—God prefers to use me in weakness rather than in strength! Many are called to this same challenge today. If God has chosen you to remain ill, will your faith shine brightly to those who know you and love you? Will you take hold of eternal life, and by your faith touch the hearts of others as they view God's eternal light through the lens of your suffering?

If God does not heal you physically, He will give you a spiritual blessing that is unmatched by anything on this earth!

Look at the power in the words Peter uses to describe our eternal hope:

> Blessed be the God and Father of our Lord Jesus Christ! According to his great mercy, he has caused us to be born again to a living hope through the resurrection of Jesus Christ from the dead, to an inheritance that is imperishable, undefiled, and unfading, kept in heaven for you, who by God's power are being guarded through faith for a salvation ready to be revealed in the last time. In this you rejoice, though now for a little while, if necessary, you have been grieved by various trials, so that the tested genuineness of your faith—more precious than gold that perishes though it is tested by fire—may be found to result in praise and glory and honor at the revelation of Jesus Christ. Though you have not seen him, you love him. Though you do not now see him, you believe in him and rejoice with joy that is inexpressible and filled with glory, obtaining the outcome of your faith, the salvation of your souls.
>
> 1 Peter 1:3-9

REJOICE IN HOPE, KNOWING THAT YOUR FUTURE SHINES BRIGHT IN THE HEAVENLY REALM!

While you are alive, your example shines with God's

power to those around you! If you cannot be healed, take a few moments for your tears! Then let the peace of God fill your heart as you look toward the glorious resurrection of eternal life.

We must examine the depth of the promise of Christ in Matthew 11:28-30. It is in Christ alone that we find rest, but there is also a yoke:

> Come to me, all who labor and are heavy laden, and I will give you rest. Take my yoke upon you, and learn from me, for I am gentle and lowly in heart, and you will find rest for your souls. For my yoke is easy, and my burden is light.

Jesus said, my burden is light and my yoke is easy. In this great passage the word *yoke* is used twice. I believe there's a reason for that specific word. You see, a yoke had two purposes when it was used on a team of oxen. First, it was designed to allow the animals to share the load. Neither animal was required to carry more that it could handle. The second purpose for the yoke was to allow the master complete control over the movements of the oxen.

When God says no to your prayers for healing, and you are so weary that you think you cannot bear the load any longer, it's time to look to your brothers and sisters in the church. We must gain strength as we share one another's burdens. In your church family, everyone has a burden! It may not be an illness, but I can assure you that each and every one of your brothers and sisters has some struggle in his or her life!

Take some time this week to consider God's purpose in your life. Is it possible that your pain and suffering could result in your greatest service to God? Could it even provide you with inner peace and joy?

- Have your friends prayed with you and thus had their own spirits lifted?
- Has your illness opened doors for you to share your faith with people who have similar struggles?
- Have people commented on your strength?
- What surprising new possibilities for ministry have opened up for you because of your suffering?

13

WHEN YOU'RE COMPLETELY HELPLESS, LOOK TOWARD GOD

JOB'S STORY

"When life knocks you down, roll over and look at the stars."

Author unknown

Then Job arose and tore his robe and shaved his head and fell on the ground and worshiped. And he said, "Naked I came from my mother's womb, and naked shall I return. The Lord gave, and the Lord has taken away; blessed be the name of the Lord." In all this Job did not sin or charge God with wrong.

Job 1:20-22

Then his wife said to him, "Do you still hold fast your integrity? Curse God and die." But he said to her, "You speak as one of the foolish women would speak. Shall we receive good from God, and shall we not receive evil?" In all this Job did not sin with his lips.

Job 2:9-10

Job had reached the end of his rope! He had lost his wealth, his children, and his health; his friends had turned against him, and even his wife had told him to curse God and die. Many of us, in the midst of a stressful time, have felt like the only thing left to do is let out a pain-filled scream and give up. So what can we do when we reach that point in our lives when we start thinking, "This just isn't fair! I'm trying to serve God with all my heart, but He's taking away my health!" What is the answer? How do we deal with the tragedy in our lives? As we listen to Job's despair, we find the answer:

> Behold, I go forward, but he is not there, and backward, but I do not perceive him; on the left hand when he is working, I do not behold him; he turns to the right hand, but I do not see him. But he knows the way that I take; when he has tried me, I shall come out as gold. My foot has held fast to his steps; I have kept his way and have not turned aside. I have not departed from

the commandment of his lips; I have treasured the words of his mouth more than my portion of food.

Job 23:8-12

What do you do when you cannot see God? When everything is so bad that you think there's no hope? In his desperation, Job took four incredible steps of faith.

1. HE COMPLETELY TRUSTED GOD!

He went back in his mind to everything he had learned and believed in his life. He trusted that God understood what was happening and that He was not going to leave Job alone. Job said, "He knows the way that I take; when he has tried me I shall come out as gold" (Job 23:10). Do you realize that you will win the battle? God's people never lose! He knows your beginning, your middle, and your end, and He's not about to desert you!

2. HE "HELD FAST TO THE STEPS OF GOD" (23:11).

Job knew what God expected of him. So he never wavered in his integrity.

> Then Job arose and tore his robe and shaved his head and fell on the ground and worshiped. And he said, "Naked I came from my mother's womb, and naked shall I return. The Lord gave, and the Lord has taken away; blessed be the name of the Lord." In all this Job did not sin or charge God with wrong.
>
> Job 1:20-22

During your darkest hours, are you still striving to please God? Have you ever gone to bed at night angry with God? If you read the book of Job carefully, you will see Job's discontent and even his anger at God over his plight in life. However, he is unmoved in his determination to follow God's path.

When I was involved in athletics, we used to say, "When the going gets tough, the tough get going!" When life gets tough, the faithful grow stronger!

Remember, the apostle Paul is another example of one who continued to follow God even down a path of suffering. Somehow Paul understood and accepted that God had chosen to use his suffering for His purposes rather than remove or prevent it.

> Three times I pleaded with the Lord about this [his thorn in the flesh], that it should leave me. But he said

to me, "My grace is sufficient for you, for my power is made perfect in weakness." Therefore I will boast all the more gladly of my weaknesses, so that the power of Christ may rest upon me.

2 Corinthians 12:8-9

Did you hear that? God's power is made perfect in our weakness! There is no greater servant of God than the individual who is chronically ill and yet is still doing good for others every single day! We are the light of the world when God's love shines through our weakness.

Job didn't completely understand what God had in mind, but he was willing to follow God's footsteps wherever they took him.

3. JOB REFUSED TO TURN AWAY FROM GOD!

He did not "turn aside" (Job 23:11). It's just downright hard to wake up hurting every single day, especially when you begin to realize that God is not answering your prayers for healing. When is enough, enough? Never! You belong to God, and He has said that He will never leave you! How long did Job suffer? We don't know, but even from the bottom of the ash heap, after all his friends had deserted him and his wife had challenged him to desert God and die, Job refused to turn away from God. The next time your disease overpowers you, look upward toward God, thank Him for the eternal life of joy that is prepared for you, and refuse to turn away from Him. It will not be easy; it will take all of your courage!

4. JOB TREASURED THE WORDS OF GOD IN HIS HEART.

What incredible power there is in the Word of God! There is light, there is joy, there is wisdom, there is shelter, there is a life-changing power that is found only in God's Word. Read it, memorize it, repeat it over and over in your prayers, and feel its healing strength.

> In the beginning was the Word, and the Word was with God, and the Word was God. He was in the beginning with God. All things were made through him, and without him was not any thing made that was made. In him was life, and the life was the light of men.
>
> John 1:1-4

Treasure God's Word in your heart. In His Word, you will find the Savior, and in the Savior, you will find life—not life for a few years on this earth, but eternal life with God in heaven!

Decide today to do these four things:

1. I will trust God's direction for my life, even when it leads me to suffering and hardship.

Shadrach, Meshach, and Abednego answered and said to the king, "O Nebuchadnezzar, we have no need to answer you in this matter. If this be so, our God whom we serve is able to deliver us from the burning fiery furnace, and he will deliver us out of your hand, O king. But if not, be it known to you, O king, that we will not serve your gods or worship the golden image that you have set up."

Daniel 3:16-18

2. I will never turn away from God's path.

For my thoughts are not your thoughts, neither are your ways my ways, declares the Lord. For as the heavens are higher than the earth, so are my ways higher than your ways and my thoughts than your thoughts. For as the rain and the snow come down from heaven and do not return there but water the earth, making it bring forth and sprout, giving seed to the sower and bread to the eater, so shall my word be that goes out from my mouth; it shall not return to me empty, but it shall accomplish that which I purpose, and shall succeed in the thing for which I sent it. For you shall go out in joy and be led forth in peace; the mountains and the hills before you shall break forth into singing, and all the trees of the field shall clap their hands.

Isaiah 55:8-12

3. I will never allow anything to turn me away from God.

Then Peter said in reply, "See, we have left everything and followed you. What then will we have?" Jesus said to them, "Truly, I say to you, in the new world, when the Son of Man will sit on his glorious throne, you who have followed me will also sit on twelve thrones, judging the twelve tribes of Israel. And everyone who has left houses or brothers or sisters or father or mother or children or lands, for my name's sake, will receive a hundredfold and will inherit eternal life.

Matthew 19:27-29

4. I will study and treasure God's Word every day.

Your word is a lamp to my feet and a light to my path. I have sworn an oath and confirmed it, to keep your righteous rules. I am severely afflicted; give me life, O Lord, according to your word! Accept my freewill offerings of praise, O Lord, and teach me your rules. I hold my life in my hand continually, but I do not forget your law. The wicked have laid a snare for me, but I do not stray from your precepts. Your testimonies are my heritage forever, for they are the joy of my heart. I incline my heart to perform your statutes forever, to the end.

Psalm 119:105-112

14

CHRIST IN YOU, THE HOPE OF GLORY

To them God chose to make known how great among the Gentiles are the riches of the glory of this mystery, which is Christ in you, the hope of glory.

Colossians 1:27

Whenever you say to yourself, I just can't go on; this is too hard. The pain is unbearable; my strength is gone, it's time to look at your real strength! It is the strength of Christ living in you. You can and you will endure the suffering and glorify Christ, not because of your strength but because of His! Let's take a careful look at the power of the one who lives within us.

HE IS GREATER THAN ANGELS

The power that lives in us is greater than the angels!

> He is the radiance of the glory of God and the exact imprint of his nature, and he upholds the universe by the word of his power. After making purification for sins, he sat down at the right hand of the Majesty on high, having become as much superior to angels as the name he has inherited is more excellent than theirs.
>
> Hebrews 1:3-4

This statement simply blows my mind. Just think of it: The radiance of God's glory, the exact imprint of God's nature, the one who is greater than the angels, lives in us. When we realize God's power is working in us, we develop a completely new perspective.

Have you ever really considered the power of God's angels? Take a look in the book of 2 Kings as King Hezekiah is trapped in the city of Jerusalem. Sennacherib's Assyrian army has surrounded the city. Hezekiah and his people are defenseless; there is no possible way of escape—at least not until Hezekiah opens up to God in prayer. He lays before God the letter sent to him by the Assyrians. In response to Hezekiah's prayer, God sends one angel. Notice the singular form of the word angel. One angel destroys 185,000 soldiers in the Assyrian army.

> And that night the angel of the Lord went out and struck down 185,000 in the camp of the Assyrians. And when people arose early in the morning, behold, these were all dead bodies. Then Sennacherib king of Assyria departed and went home and lived at Nineveh.
>
> 2 Kings 19:35-36

Jesus Christ is greater than the angels, and His power lives in you. His power is there to accomplish God's will for your life and give you eternal life! Remember, our blessings are not the short-term blessings of this earth; they are eternal!

HE IS GREATER THAN MOSES

The one living in you, Jesus Christ, is greater than Moses. Yes, within you is a power greater than the great lawgiver of the Old Testament—Moses, the one who led the Israelite nation out of slavery, the one who went up Mount Sinai and met personally with God as He delivered the Ten Commandments.

The man who led a nation for forty years is nothing compared with Jesus Christ.

> Therefore, holy brothers, you who share in a heavenly calling, consider Jesus, the apostle and high priest of our confession, who was faithful to him who appointed him, just as Moses also was faithful in all God's house. For Jesus has been counted worthy of more glory than Moses—as much more glory as the builder of a house has more honor than the house itself.
>
> Hebrews 3:1-3

How can we possibly say, "I just don't have enough strength to endure this pain," with Christ living in our hearts? We do have the strength! We do have the will! We do have the courage! We will accomplish God's purpose in our lives!

HE IS THE GREAT HIGH PRIEST

Believe it or not, the one who lives in us, Jesus Christ, understands our suffering because He is the great high priest. The responsibility of a priest is to connect people with God. Jesus can connect us to God because He was God in the flesh.

He understands because He has suffered much more than we will ever suffer.

> Since then we have a great high priest who has passed through the heavens, Jesus, the Son of God, let us hold fast our confession. For we do not have a high priest who is unable to sympathize with our weaknesses, but one who in every respect has been tempted as we are, yet without sin. Let us then with confidence draw near to the throne of grace, that we may receive mercy and find grace to help in time of need.
>
> Hebrews 4:14-16

There's our strength! Living in us is the powerful high priest who understands us completely and never leaves the presence of God. God's grace and eternal mercy is extended through his Son. Are you beginning to see the incredible strength you have through Jesus Christ? Yes, we suffer with our illnesses, but never without the gentle hand of Jesus guiding us toward eternal peace.

> Let not your hearts be troubled. Believe in God; believe also in me. In my Father's house are many rooms. If it were not so, would I have told you that I go to prepare a place for you? And if I go and prepare a place for you, I

will come again and will take you to myself, that where I am you may be also.

John 14:1-3

In the Old Testament, only the high priest could enter into the presence of God. Before entering the Holy of Holies, on the Day of Atonement he was required to put on a holy linen garment and linen undergarments, and he was to tie a linen sash around his waist and put on a linen turban. He was to cleanse himself in water before he dressed. He took two goats as offerings. First he offered a ram for himself. Then he took the two goats before the Lord and offered one of them as a sacrifice. After the sacrifice, he went out to the congregation and presented the other goat alive, signifying God's releasing the people of their transgressions. All of these things were required for him to fulfill his responsibilities as high priest. Each year, the process had to be repeated in order to appease God.

When Jesus Christ came, all of the actions of the previous high priests were abolished. The one who lives in us has made the complete sacrifice for our sins.

> For Christ has entered, not into holy places made with hands, which are copies of the true things, but into

heaven itself, now to appear in the presence of God on our behalf.

Hebrews 9:24

- What is your present relationship with the great high priest? How does Christ impact your life right now?

My little children, I am writing these things to you so that you may not sin. But if anyone does sin, we have an advocate with the Father, Jesus Christ the righteous. He is the propitiation for our sins, and not for ours only but also for the sins of the whole world.

1 John 2:1-2

- What is the significance of Christ living in you?

That according to the riches of his glory he may grant you to be strengthened with power through his Spirit in your inner being, so that Christ may dwell in your hearts through faith—that you, being rooted and grounded in love, may have strength to comprehend with all the saints what is the breadth and length and height and depth, and to know the love of Christ that surpasses knowledge, that you may be filled with all the fullness of God.

Ephesians 3:16-19

- How has His presence helped you deal with your illness?

- How does God give us comfort through Christ? Read 2 Corinthians 1-2.

15

A BEAUTIFUL, BEAUTIFUL PAIN-FREE DAY

> Behold! I tell you a mystery. We shall not all sleep, but we shall all be changed, in a moment, in the twinkling of an eye, at the last trumpet. For the trumpet will sound, and the dead will be raised imperishable, and we shall be changed.
>
> 1 Corinthians 15:51-52

Close your eyes and take a careful look at your future: If you belong to Christ, you will wake up to a radiant day beyond anything you've ever seen! You will be amazed as you suddenly feel strong, with absolutely no pain of any kind. When you look in the mirror you will unexpectedly see your new body, which will be incredibly strong and healthy. Your appearance will be more perfect than ever before! In fact, you will be like one of the angels in heaven. You will feel vitality in every part of your body! In fact, your body will be completely different than it has ever been before. You won't really understand the feeling, or the strength or the beauty, until you look and see the beautiful city of God and realize that you are in heaven!

YOU WILL NEVER FEEL PHYSICAL PAIN AGAIN!

> He will wipe away every tear from their eyes, and death shall be no more, neither shall there be mourning, nor crying, nor pain anymore, for the former things have passed away.
>
> Revelation 21:4

If you've been in pain for years, it's hard to imagine feeling great every moment—an eternity of perfect, unchanging health. Seriously, aren't God's promises amazing? Our reward in heaven is glorious! Your joints will never creak again. You will never visit a doctor again. You will never run a fever or have a seizure or feel weakness in your muscles. All these things will be gone forever!

FREEDOM FROM EMOTIONAL PAIN!

No tears, no sorrow, no stress, no worry, no fears, no anxiety, only the joy of eternal peace! Everything you have ever worried about will be over! Gone forever!

> I have said these things to you, that in me you may have peace. In the world you will have tribulation, but take heart; I have overcome the world.
> John 16:33

A BEAUTIFUL NEW HOME

Now, as you are experiencing pain-free living in the heavenly realm, it's time to take a close look at your new home. A friend of mine, Don Schmerse, is a master builder. I'm always amazed when I look at the homes he builds and compare them with other houses. The beauty of his homes is unmistakable: the craftsmanship, the attention to detail, the careful planning and the outstanding finish work are obvious.

The Bible tells us that the builder of our house in heaven is Jesus Christ. Let's take a walk down the streets of gold and look at the house that Jesus prepared for you. It is just the right size, has just the right decorations, is perfectly color-coordinated to suit your taste, and is built to last for eternity.

> And if I go and prepare a place for you, I will come again and will take you to myself, that where I am you may be also.
>
> John 14:3

What a comfortable, warm, beautiful place to live. Just think, this is not a house that will get old or need repainting. You will never pull weeds in the garden.

NOTHING WILL EVER DECAY OR GET OLD!

I love my new car! That is, I loved it five and a half years ago when I first bought it. Now it's got almost 100,000 miles on it, along with a few scratches, and the paint doesn't look very good. It seems like everything on earth is the very best when you first get it, and then it gets old and dilapidated. Not so in heaven!

> Blessed be the God and Father of our Lord Jesus Christ! According to his great mercy, he has caused us to be born again to a living hope through the resurrection

of Jesus Christ from the dead, to an inheritance that is imperishable, undefiled, and unfading, kept in heaven for you.

1 Peter 1:3-4

NOW IT'S TIME TO MEET YOUR NEW NEIGHBORS

Giving thanks to the Father, who has qualified you to share in the inheritance of the saints in light. He has delivered us from the domain of darkness and transferred us to the kingdom of his beloved Son, in whom we have redemption, the forgiveness of sins.

Colossians 1:12-14

Yes, during our thousands of years in heaven, we will meet Paul and Barnabas, David and Jonathan, Ruth and Esther, Peter and John and all the other apostles. We can take a walk down the street and talk with Moses, Elijah, Daniel, or Jeremiah. In fact, we will have the time and the opportunity to speak with all the saints mentioned in the Bible. We will also have the opportunity to talk with Christians who lived before us and protected the truth of God's Word. Many of them were martyrs. Some of them were ordinary people like us, with their own stories to tell. Every one of us will be prepared to rejoice together in the presence of our Lord.

REJOICING TOGETHER FOR ETERNITY!

Although John's glimpse of heaven is beyond our understanding, he describes in human terms the celebration before the throne of our Lord in heaven:

> And they sang a new song, saying, "Worthy are you to take the scroll and to open its seals, for you were slain, and by your blood you ransomed people for God from every tribe and language and people and nation, and you have made them a kingdom and priests to our God, and they shall reign on the earth." Then I looked, and I heard around the throne and the living creatures and the elders the voice of many angels, numbering myriads of myriads and thousands of thousands, saying in a loud voice, "Worthy is the Lamb who was slain, to receive power and wealth and wisdom and might and honor and glory and blessing!" And I heard every creature in heaven and on earth and under the earth and in the sea, and all that is in them, saying, "To him who sits on the throne and to the lamb be blessing and honor and glory and might forever and ever!" And

the four living creatures said, "Amen!" and the elders fell down and worshiped.

Revelation 5:9-14

Can you imagine the beauty of that song? Can you contemplate the power of the voices of thousands upon thousands of angels? What an exciting celebration this will be as we look directly at our heavenly Father, Jehovah the Almighty, and his Son, Jesus Christ.

It's time to begin a brand-new way of thinking as you consider these questions:

- Would you rather have a nice home on earth or one prepared by Christ in heaven?

- Would you rather be healed to live a few years pain-free on this earth or spend eternity pain-free in heaven?

- Consider the focus of all your thoughts. Are they thoughts that will cause you to be a conqueror?

You see, the bottom line of everything we have discussed in this book is that you and I will be victorious in Christ! How can we allow ourselves to be discouraged when He gives us the ultimate victory? He will never leave us or betray us. The only way to lose our relationship with Christ is to refuse the victory He gives us. Stay faithful to Christ! And rejoice for eternity!

> Who shall separate us from the love of Christ? Shall tribulation, or distress, or persecution, or famine, or nakedness, or danger, or sword? As it is written, "For your sake we are being killed all the day long; we are regarded as sheep to be slaughtered." No, in all these things we are more than conquerors through him who loved us. For I am sure that neither death nor life, nor angels nor rulers, nor things present nor things to come, nor powers, nor height nor depth, nor anything else in all creation, will be able to separate us from the love of God in Christ Jesus our Lord.
>
> Romans 8:35-39

As an insulin dependent diabetic for fifty years, Dean Kilmer has been able to identify with individuals struggling with illness and stress. While serving as a minister, he has had the opportunity to work with, and be encouraged by, hundreds of faithful people who are serving God in spite of their struggles.

Dean is a graduate of Harding University and has a Master's degree from Abilene Christian University. He has been married to his wife, Karen, for 46 years; they have two married children and five grandchildren.

Please share your faith story with others
at: www.deankilmer.com/share

www.ingramcontent.com/pod-product-compliance
Lightning Source LLC
Chambersburg PA
CBHW070055120526
44588CB00033B/1460